TO : _____

FROM : _____

Providing HOPE and ENCOURAGEMENT for adults
and children. May this book help our next generation
design their lives and their place in the world.

DESIGNING LIVES:
INSPIRING OUR CHILDREN TODAY TO INSPIRE OUR WORLD TOMORROW

DESIREE K. WILLIAMS

WESTBOW
P R E S S®
A DIVISION OF THOMAS NELSON
& ZONDERVAN

WestBow Press books may be ordered through booksellers or by contacting:

WestBow Press
A Division of Thomas Nelson & Zondervan
1663 Liberty Drive
Bloomington, IN 47403
www.westbowpress.com
1 (866) 928-1240

ISBN: 978-1-9736-8889-1 (sc)
ISBN: 978-1-9736-8888-4 (e)

Print information available on the last page.

WestBow Press rev. date: 04/13/2020

CONTENTS

Dedication vii

Introduction xi

PART I: IT BEGINS AT HOME

Activity Sheet 1 1

  It Begins At Home 2

  Bonding is Beneficial 4

  Making History... Today 6

  Activities Count! 8

PART II: THE SCHOOL CHALLENGE

College Countdown Chart ~ Grades 9-12 13

  Expand Horizons 15

  Activities Count! 19

PART III: HELPING CHILDREN HAVE A VISION

Activity Sheet 2 23

  Back To Basics And Moving Forward, *message by Mary G. Johnson* ...24

  Helping Children Have A Vision 27

Conclusions 29

When I Designed My World, *poem by Author*.....................................31

Notes...35

DEDICATION

This book is dedicated to my sons Matthew, Evan, and Emmanuel (Manny) who continue to teach and inspire me. I thank God for each of you and look forward to seeing how God will show Himself through your individual callings, gifts, talents and abilities. Continue to be an inspiration and light in the world. I love you.

I would also like to thank my mother, Mary G. Johnson for always believing in me. She has always been "the wings beneath my wings", my biggest supporter, and biggest fan. Happy Mother's Day, Mom. I love you.

We will not hide them from their children, but (we will) tell to the generation to come the praiseworthy deeds of the LORD. And (tell of) His great might and power and the wonderful works that He has done.

That the generation to come might know them, that the children still to be born may arise and recount them to their children, That they should set place their confidence in God and not forget the works of God, but keep His commandments

-Psalms 78:4,6-7 (AMP)

INTRODUCTION

As a mother today, I am beginning to realize how important our foundation training plays in our overall makeup. Our experiences, values, and influences all make an impact – negatively and/or positively – on us and subsequently on our children.

Take a look back at your own upbringing. How has it influenced you today? I can recall one of my most treasured of all well-wishes written in my high school yearbook came from my mother. She wrote of a "Dream Voyage." Her valedictorian address to the Class of 1955 expressed how our dreams conceived can and will be achieved without question. She charged me... I could not wait to take the world by storm!

How can we pass the torch to future generations without the fire going out?

I would like to think that we, the parent and child, dream, discover and journey to get to a destination together. The children with their own unique set of ideas and goals of what they desire to contribute to the world when they grow up- charting the course.

Developed in three parts to help us determine our children's role and parental responsibility, the goal of this book is to assist the families in their desire to provide a clearer, brighter and more successful future for our generations to come.

- **Part One: "It Begins At Home"** addresses fundamental focuses on ideas and solutions for family/ home relations. The core of any child's nurturing development.

- **Part Two: "The School Challenge"** gives us a window into our education system and how our children can get the most out of it.
- **Part Three: "Helping Children Have a VISION"** challenges industry to pay close attention to the work force of the future. Roll up its sleeves and lend a hand.

Take hold of instruction; (actively seek it, grip it firmly and) do not let go. Guard her, for she is your life.
-Proverbs 4:13 (AMP)

PART I

It Begins at Home

Train up a child in the way he should go (teaching him to seek God's wisdom and will for his abilities and talents), Even when he is old he will not depart from it.
-Proverbs 22:6 (AMP)

ACTIVITY SHEET 1

What I Want to Be When I Grow Up

Today's Date: _____

My grade and age: _____

Things that interest me: _____

_____

_____

_____

These are my strengths/things I do well at: _____

_____

_____

_____

What I want to be when I grow up: _____

_____

_____

_____

Why I want to be this: _____

_____

_____

_____

IT BEGINS AT HOME

"It begins at home." It seems that hardly a week goes by where I do not hear these words on television or read them in a newspaper or magazine article. Most of them are being spoken by a politician or an agency head. Most often they are speaking angry responses to the many problems being caused by today's misguided youth. Sadly, it is much less often that I hear or read in the media of a proud parent having an opportunity to state, "It beings at home..."

There is not an agency or governmental structure created that is greater in power and influence than the family. The statement, "I cannot imagine a more challenging, yet rewarding responsibility," in the context of raising a family is very true.

Witnessing various stages of growth and development within our children gives us a sense of joy and accomplishment that cannot be measured by dollars. Faith, discipline, loving and encouragement are just some of the priceless jewels which can influence the nurturing process.

Throughout history, the home and family have been the foundation for every society, no matter the cultural background. Having an active role in our children's lives is imperative to their overall being. The home must be the first empowering environment which fosters a well-rounded, positive, happy upbringing. By good example, and by clean upright moral standards, good parenting is the most influential resource to date.

We are all aware of our limitations, but that is not the legacy, nor the focus we want to pass down to our children. Helping them dare to dream in spite of the inevitable obstacles of life should be our challenge! How else will they strive toward their desired destination? When we are not willing to accept this challenge, the evidence is clear.

If there is not a healthy, supportive, positive outlook to reading and learning at home, how can we expect our children to enjoy and get the most out of the entire educational experience at school?

Parenting does begin at home!

Through (skillful and godly) wisdom a house (a life, a home, a family) is built, And by understanding it is established (on a sound and good foundation),...

-Proverbs 24:3 (AMP)

BONDING IS BENEFICIAL

Much like adults who evolve socially, emotionally, and intellectually, children experience a variety of stages also. Ages 0-5 years are considered the most precious and fundamental stage –formulating ideas and opinions, which remain with them for the rest of their lives.

- **Talking** to children as early as in-utero is a great time to being the lifelong relationship with our children. Singing and reading also aid in our children knowing and trusting, feeling secure and protected, calm and reassured.

- **Encouragement** is vitally important to our children's overall adjusting. Fostering confidence and curiosity at an early age plays a considerable role in how experiences are received and displayed.

- **Sharing** in our children's lives respectfully as friendships are made, interest change, likes and dislikes are expressed and accepting their individual personalities is key to parent-child relations. Studies show repeatedly that the more communicative the family, the less likely children are to seek attention, good or bad, outside of the home. This form of nurturing is priceless. Later on as an adolescent or young adults, sharing prepares them for healthy interaction in school, work and relating with others. My children are very happy to learn about my childhood experiences and we often reminisce on them.

- **Listening** is an art of any age! Where do most children find themselves later on if they have not learned this art? How to "listen and being listened to" go hand-in-hand".

- **Playing Games** with our children is perhaps the greatest training tool available for parents. It is often said, "Children are master imitators" and how we interact with them today is essentially how they will interact with other tomorrow.

MAKING HISTORY... TODAY

In today's society, children are being bombarded with situations that many adults have never had to encounter—and cannot begin to comprehend. It is quite understandable that, face with such challenges, a child may become lost. Peer pressures, family, economic turmoil, societal stress, to name a few.

As written in the proverbs of King Solomon of ancient Israel, "*Train up a child in the way he should go and he will never depart from it.*" Parents today have the unique responsibility, virtually forgotten by some, to teach knowledge, reverence for God, common sense, self-control, and good manners. To be role models for our children ourselves. "We can do no wrong," some might say in reference to a child's love for its parents. Who we are, where we came from, and what came before are all essential pieces to a child's identity. History of family traditions, music, foods, philosophies and spiritual beliefs all bond our children to their heritage and what part they play in it. Let us not forget to train our children. Giving them a loving sense of pride and belonging—can any gift be greater?

> ** He who learns from instruction and correction is on the (right) path of life (and for others his example is a path toward wisdom and blessing), But he who ignores and refuses correction goes off course (and for others his example is a path toward sin and ruin).*
>
> -Proverbs 10:17 (AMP)

If grandparents are distant or gone, keep their memories alive through pictures, storytelling, etc. If quilt-making or preserving fruit or fly fishing and baseball were a part of your upbringing, return the gift to your children! Tragically, in some cases, there were no role models which stood out. In that case, introduce your children to the library where an exhaustive array of heroes exist! Certain characters can assist us in helping our children foster courage, faith, strength, character, imagination, goals or just plain rumor!

Our heritage offers many things to us and our children and there should be no fear or intimidation in expressing such. Math, astronomy, medicine, art, music, poetry—the list is endless and our children's contributions are eagerly anticipated. They need to know this and they need to hear this from the parents. Every strong nation is built upon something called "dreams" and legacy building begins with honoring them. Dream! Dream Big!

ACTIVITIES COUNT!

Seasonal, Social and Cultural Excursions are a great deal of family fun. They renew you. Train yourself and the children not to become "chained" to the Internet. There is a lot going on in the world—why settle for a picture when you can experience the entire view!

Zoos, Museums and Libraries are always exciting and adventurous with their various puppet shows, storytelling, arts and crafts events and highlight guests and animals. Local newspapers carry a variety of events for all ages to participate in on a weekly monthly basis.

National and Overseas Trips are also a great way to expand our children's minds, vocabulary, goals and visions for themselves.

Service. There can never be enough of it, and the rewards to both the giver and receiver are immeasurable. When children are encouraged (mostly through the example set by their parents) to spend quality time "giving" instead of concentrating on "getting," their overall perspective on life is improved. Look back and remember what your own grandparents and parents were involved in that was positive. Their appreciation seemed to spill over into your joy also, did it not?

Serving and delivering meals or clothing and toys to the needy can be a rewarding family experience. Spending time with the elderly are just a few examples of purposeful activities we can all do more of together.

The Church today is evolving. The Church (a gathering; an assembly of believers) is realizing that our youth are "falling away" at record numbers and is creating ways to foster their hopes, promote positive change, and build lifelong bonds. It takes a village to raise a child, but it takes the church to empower a family.

Churches today are not only interested in teaching members for spiritual education, baptism, individual witnessing to convert other believers, and encouraging service in outreach missions, but they are also coming alongside their members. The once traditional family is now enlarged to be identified as single-parent households, grandparents raising their grandchildren, "children" themselves rearing children, runaway youth living with others...

The Church along with other agencies are standing in the ever-widening gap of family brokenness. They are not only exposing the ills of the world, but they offer a sanctuary where people may reach out to other people and ease each other's burdens, celebrate one another's victories, and learn how to grow stronger—together. Our children need to know where they can go for all the support that is there in the Church in abundance (if indeed that Church is a healthy one). There they find mentorship, counseling, financial assistance, spiritual support, and strength to counteract negative influences with peers of like mind.

A home away from home with doors and open arms that are always warm and inviting. Children need to be directed both how to interact "in" the world and how to conduct themselves "apart" from the world. Where else can they learn the contrast?

Today, churches are not relying on the school systems to provide all the necessary scholastic skill-building needed to support the character development that is being fostered in Sunday school and youth-church activities.

Nurturing well-rounded spirit-filled leaders for tomorrow, many churches are producing their own academic curriculums, study skill booklets, positive alternative music which caters to the youth market, youth seminars, Bible-based summer camps, and conducting in-house college prep courses and tutorial services, which all round, out a child's foundational years. Growing up I looked forward to the weekends. My family calendar was always full of activities (beside the chores) like volleyball practice down at Church, bus trips to Pennsylvania for Christmas shopping, and an ole colonial style-lunch. These are the memories that I would like to share now with my children.

Give instruction to a wise man and he will become even wiser;
Teach a righteous man and he will increase his learning.
-Proverbs 9:9 (AMP)

PART II

The School Challenge

The wise will hear and increase their learning,
And the person of understanding will acquire wise counsel and
the skill (to steer his course wisely and lead others to the truth)—
-Proverbs 1:5 (AMP)

COLLEGE COUNTDOWN CHART

9th Grade

- Focus on getting good grades! Your GPA starts now
- Register on scholarship websites
- Get involved in a variety of activities to find out what interests you

* FAMILY VACATIONS – Visit Colleges/Take Tours

10th Grade

- Create a Dream Wall in your bedroom
- Make good grades a priority – your GPA continues to grow
- Register at scholarship websites
- Take the PLAN (practice ACT) test in October
- Start thinking about careers that interest you
- Continue to participate in extracurricular activities

* FAMILY VACATIONS – Visit Colleges/Take Tours

11th Grade

- Remember, 2nd semester GPA goes on your applications!
- Attend college fairs (see calendar for dates).
- Take the PSAT in October

- Make a list of about 10 potential colleges
- Meet with the college representatives that visit your school
- Utilize your two college days
- Start thinking about possible majors
- Get involved in a variety of areas – it helps to be well-rounded
- Plan to take the ACT test by June (you can do this multiple times)

* FAMILY VACATIONS – Visit Colleges/Take Tours

12th Grade

- Grades still matter. Schools require a final transcript
- Attend college fairs (see calendar for dates)
- Choose a general area of study (assists in college selection)
- Utilize your two college days
- Narrow your choices to the top five schools
- Send applications by December
- Take the ACT until you are satisfied, but no later than December!
- File your FAFSA form (January)
- Meet with the college representatives that come to your school
- Register at scholarships websites

EXPAND HORIZONS

As parents, it is fundamentally important that we are always aware of what is available for our children (examples: tutorial programs, internships, workshops). They cannot achieve this by themselves. Monitoring your own child progress in partnership with faculty and advisors throughout his/her school careers can be beneficial to ensuring your own child is not "left behind."

A decade earlier, Education Secretary Richard Riley was quoted as saying, "Teachers cannot carry the load of being part-time social workers, family counselors, and police officers." How much more can be said today!

Teachers own lives hang in the balance with ever-threatening budget cuts, wage cuts, expanded class sizes, and higher individual student performance expectations with limited supplies to do it! (I am sure you have noticed, like I have, the student required school supply list gets longer with each passing year...)

Along "with" faculty, parents are charged to help their children to be prepared and to aspire for greatness in life and industry and service to others. Knowing our own children and helping teachers know them and identify where they are and where they can be by the end of the school year is a move in the right direction for the best desired results.

Listed below is an example outlining the importance of knowing our own children and how we can best guide them into a happy rewarding planned future instead of a future fallen into.

I. Child's Interest

clothes shopping, talking on phone, video games

II. Scholastic Strengths and Talents

art, computer science, history, math, Computer Aided Design (CAD) etc.

III. H.S./College Major & Minor Subjects

design, marketing, accounting, Graphic Designer, Business Administration, etc.

IV. Internships, Employment

research assistant, lab technician, instructor, marketing, sales rep, teaching assistant, counselor etc.

V. Career Opportunities! (open and diverse)

stronger specialization opportunities etc.

This diagram teaches goal-setting. Helping children chart their course as early as possible from the beginning; making necessary adjustments as needed, and staying focused on getting to the desired destination are just a few helpful hints to getting them on their way for a successful life. Creating a plan, from the beginning of interest and curiosity, how to get from point A to point B.

Children are unique and special. Their talents are their gifts to share with mankind. Watch for and cultivate them.

I. **Children's Interests** present themselves early and most do not appear to be of any significance, as time goes on parents begin to see definite patterns. What they are continuously drawn to—support if positive. Periodically comment on how much you admire them for a certain achievement, providing reinforcing literature, or clipping articles on a particular subject of interest are just a few ways parents can become involved, and keep their child's interests alive.

II. Scholastic Strengths and Talents become more evident and stronger with each passing year. Through testing and evaluating grades, a view into what our children favor is made clear. Collectively, parents and faculty can assist children through encouragement, time, attention, and an inviting open door for communication. Ask questions.

While talking to your children, prepare them to think about their future plans. Which schools offer the most comprehensive programs of interest? How would your major/minor subjects best help you reach and attain your desired goal? Is there a conference or seminar or discovery camp you would like to attend? Are there additional reading materials or websites available to investigate further? Attentively listen to responses. Help them think through a thought more thoroughly. (Can you say that three times?)

III. High School/College—Major/Minor Subjects. While high school and college courses are carefully being reviewed and chosen, students need to be advised by parents not to feel pressure to "lock-in" to a particular field of study too lightly. Leave room to grow, pay attention, and continue enlarging their view of all they can be. Guide them toward training with realistic future opportunities and growth potential.

Today's society is filled with Master's and Doctorate degree individuals who are so specialized and narrow in focus that the jobs sought after are few in number. Entire industries have moved overseas and many dreams were lost; options slim.

Minor subjects are a "major" deal. Outside prep courses as well as internships need the student's full attention. Through investigation and communication our children are off to a tremendous start!

IV. Internships. Adopting mentors in related fields puts our children at a higher advantage. Having them seek summer employment or volunteering at a firm develops not only their business skills but social skills and dress etiquette as well.

Industry doors open more readily, resumes are strengthened, and professional references can always help our young people climb the ladder of success faster. The more you know—the more you grow!

V. Career Opportunities! Today's dreamers are tomorrow's leaders. The classroom of life (or a success-filled life) begins while we are young. Reminding our children to remain focused on "the bigger picture" will keep them on board for the duration of their journey. How many have "jobs" today instead of "careers"? When students embark on their journey outside the safe walls of school, parents can, again assist them in considering the strengths and talents FIRST! What greater asset can an employer ask for in an employee above their expertise in a particular skill—than to love their job performance attitude also.

- more vacation destinations
- more museums to visit
- more books to purchase
- and greater understanding of how to help our children with educational opportunities and course specialization (i.e. Physics, Mathematics, Biology and Geology)

Ask and keep on asking and it will be given to you; seek and keep on seeking and you will find; knock and keep on knocking and the door will be opened to you.

-Matthew 7:7 (AMP)

ACTIVITIES COUNT!

Clubs and Teams outside or inside the school system are always a plus to awakening a child's talents and abilities. They are character, confidence, and energy building. Could it be that is all the youth in gangs today are seeking—but found it in the wrong place? An atmosphere where they could have shared themselves in some positive way, having attention and acceptance amongst their peers that they were not finding primarily in a home/family environment?

Exposing our children to healthy alternatives available in most areas allow them to invite the "right" people into their lives from the beginning. Morale, leadership, and values are all reinforced through extracurricular activities.

PART III

Helping Children Have a Vision

*A man's gift (given in love or courtesy) makes room for him
And brings him before great men.*
-Proverbs 18:16 (AMP)

ACTIVITY SHEET 2

DRAW the VISION
WRITE the VISION

HANG IT UP!

* Write the VISION... Hang it up... It will surely come to pass

~ Habakkuk 2:2-3

BACK TO BASICS AND MOVING FORWARD

By Mary Goodwine Johnson

As I look back over the past years of my life (I am now in my 83rd year), I became astutely aware of the many changes that came about in every aspect in its history. I particularly focused on parenting and child rearing as it was then and how it is done now. It led me to what I consider could be valuably gleaned from all aspects of those things that were needed to accomplish the best of the basic foundational aspects and those structures needed today to go forward in directing and challenging how we pass on those requirements to our youth. I concluded that the basic foundations are still important, and going forward, it dictates that firm structural teachings, built upon those foundations are much needed today.

Therefore, I beseech you parents to encompass some of the following into your formulated plan going forward in what to include into your manual of child rearing.

I foresee and predict, that the future of our families and that of our upcoming generations will make a profound impact on our Nation and the world. In order to accomplish this, we must prepare our children and children's children to choose their paths in life correctly. This preparation begins in the home. It is the very first introduction into the world. Here the training begins into the minds and everyday encounter of a small child's mind. It is here that whatever the child sees, hears, is subjected to, cause a lasting impression.

Introduce your child to Jesus the Christ, starting with the "child's prayer "Now I lay me down to sleep…" Teach and train carefully. It is here that you begin the charting and mapping of your child's pathway through life.

Secondly, the next training away from home is the Church. Remember, when a child is introduced to God at a very young age, he/she would never depart from who God is and their relationship with Him would continue to grow. Reinforcing what the child has learned in the home, is the introduction of Bible study, the learning and understanding of Bible verses, and the listening to of Bible stories and interactions with others in a Spiritual way. The child will become exposed to those things of God; good attitudes, and learning to be even more courteous, even to strangers; kindness, knowing how to treat others in a manner that is acceptable even by God; commitment, accepting and following through on whatever task is entrusted into one's care; showing a caring and loving attitude toward both God and neighbor (which includes neighbors far and wide – not just in your immediate surrounding, but worldwide).

Third, education must be of the highest standard. Meaning, teach the child to set his/her goals high and work diligently to achieve them. Even though a college education is not always achievable for whatever reason, encourage your child to pursue goals that will educate and prepare to be able to provide care for his/herself or others also if necessary. Looking back on my years, there were available many training schools other than colleges. I, myself, did not go to college right after high school even though I was valedictorian of my class of "55." But, after the births of all four of my children, I obtained my Bachelor of Science degree while working full time nights and attending college full time days.

With enough training and encouragement, you can coax a child into adapting a certain "state of mind" that would help that child chart a road to success. The child must believe within itself that "If I put my mind to it I can achieve it. Anything in life that someone else can do, I can do also, if I set my goal to that which I aspire and set my goal high enough. If the child is going to college/university, for which I recommend, encourage that child to obtain as high a degree that he/she can possibly obtain. This is the world we live in today, no longer is a high school diploma or associates degree getting one to where one could live comfortably in today's society. The higher the degree, the better opportunity to achieve accomplished desires.

Fourth, Teach your child that adversaries are a definitive part of life, they must and will deal with it regardless of what happens going forward! The child must know that each challenge in life is a life lesson, how one deals with them is how well one learns to cope and move forward. This is a part of God's plan. You live and you learn. You cannot learn anything of value, if everything comes easy and you do not learn how and when to solve problems and how to think through adverse circumstances. And, most of all, learning to depend on God to get you through them. Adversaries is a part of life, it's a part of the mechanics that help you navigate through and grow, making you grow stronger as you encounter each challenge you face each day.

Lastly, but, not all of what you can teach your child, is exposing him/her to the finer things of life: the arts, museums, the political arena, travel, advancement in medical discoveries, financial stability, charity work, a variety of things that would help your child chart his/her course on the pathway through life. Also, teaching the child about change. If there is one assurance in life, it is that we will experience change, as I have. In fact, change is the very substance of life. I couldn't begin to tell you how many changes I have experienced while going through every aspect of my life! Change is the force that moves life forward. We must learn and teach our children to welcome change and not resist it.

So, let us, as parents, build a better world by using our strength and character, our prodigious energy and unflagging determination to parent our children and encourage them to do what it takes to do the hard work required, sustain a strong belief in their abilities, and have an unshakeable conviction that this world in which we live in is worth both their and our effort to make it a better place.

HELPING CHILDREN HAVE A VISION

One could say the first "page" in the journey of a young person's life comes at Graduation Day. I can recall feelings of excitement of having finally arrived and wondering where I was going next. There was a lot of preparation going into that day and during my journey. I had a lot of help. My mother supported my interests and my siblings always had an encouraging word. It was because I was guided on what to bring (positive attitude), what to erase (negative influence), how to get through the "sketchy" times (trials), and how to get back on course when I felt lost or tired—that I made it to my desired destination. A successful rewarding life and career, just as I had planned from my youth. Doing what I always DESIGNED in my mind to accomplish. Many more than I care to admit became lost and overwhelmed; locked out of life the way it was intended for lack of direction, support and encouragement in areas of talent and skill. Opportunities available today for "all" children are only being taken advantage of and benefitting the "few."

Today's market still dictates that "only the strong will survive." Each month jobs by the thousands are being lost, and children see their futures as dim where once it was looked at brightly. Industry preparation can and should address these issues. Many of our youth are feeling the employment markets' negative effects within their own homes. Concentration once focused on studies alone has been declining for years towards "quick fix" alternatives like "dropping-out," "hanging out," and "pouring out" drugs into neighboring communities. Parents, tomorrow is only a moment away. Let us help our children realize they have been specially designed by God to make a positive contribution in their generation. Teach them to celebrate their uniqueness. Do not let them become lost. Challenge industry to answer our children's cry for guidance and opportunity.

> Commit your works to the Lord (submit and trust them to Him), And your plans will succeed (if you respond to His will and guidance).
>
> -Proverbs 16:3 (AMP)

Here are some tips on how to get started and how to encourage industry to help. They should create:

- More open-house tours.
- Donations of time and money to support more schools on the elementary and middle school levels.
- Create more summer jobs for youth.
- Recycle trade magazines to local school libraries and classrooms.
- Donate computers, books.
- Establish local school scholarships.
- Support neighborhood school athletic teams, scholastic clubs, and summer camps.
- Support existing school programs.
- Assist in creating tomorrow's leaders in under developed communities.

Information. We must get it and use it!

CONCLUSIONS

As an adult today my mind constantly races on "what is next to do?" It makes life fun and challenging to have goals and set out to accomplish them—going higher and higher. I am not sure where the energy comes from (although I have an idea… smile!). It has been a way of life from my youth, and I cannot get away from it. It is the only way I know.

If our lives were not about moving forward, being fulfilled, constantly growing, celebrating and embracing change, encouraging others to do the same—then where would our enjoyment come from?

I ask myself often, how can I help my children on their journey, but more importantly I ASK THEM—not once but on a regular basis. There might be changes so adjustments are made. Together we go about creating a masterpiece life for them full of happiness. It does not take a high-intellect to accomplish something—just high expectations and good old-fashioned work to get the most out of life. I would like *all* children to live a full, rewarding life with plenty of good memories and enriching experiences to pass on and assist the generations behind them…

To me—that is true success.
Good luck, Parents. Enjoy the Journey!

The beginning of wisdom is: Get (skillful and godly) wisdom (it is preeminent)! And with all your acquiring, get understanding (actively seek spiritual discernment, mature comprehension, and logical interpretation).

-Proverbs 4:7 (AMP)

WHEN I DESIGNED MY WORLD

When I Designed My World
The White House was transparent
the activity inside was clear
National leaders came together
praying
That OUR LORD would soon
appear!

When I Designed My World
They admitted and we submitted
to ourselves and one another
We need the Savior
to curb our Nation's behavior.

When I Designed My World
Repentance was worldwide
The Far East would befriend the
West
Russia would embrace the U.S.
and along with Europe share all they
possessed
with AFRICA and HAITI.

When I Designed My World
Morning came, the sun rose
my slumber for the night was through
I awoke joyful, peaceful, happy,
smiling—
Realizing it was all TRUE!
When I Designed My World

-Desireé Williams

What I Want to Be When I Grow Up

DREAM. EXPLORE. LEARN. SOAR.

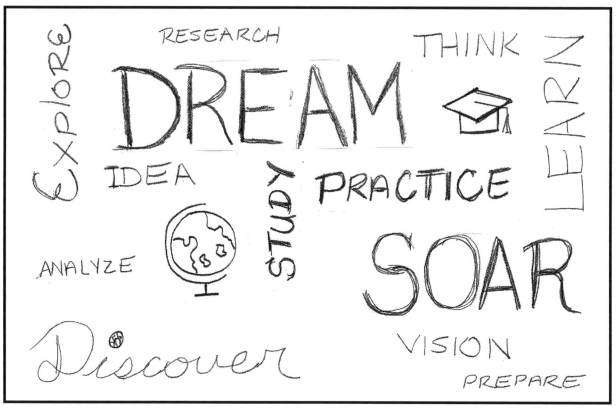

© Desireé K. Williams

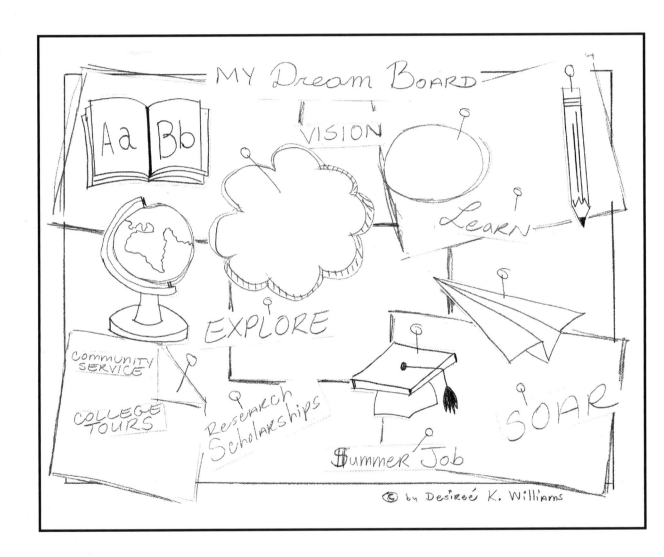

NOTES

Family Vacations
College Tours

Family Vacations
College Tours

Family Vacations
College Tours

DREAM

EXPLORE

LEARN

SOAR

Printed in the United States
By Bookmasters